50 World Curries You Must Try

By: Kelly Johnson

Table of Contents

- Indian Butter Chicken Curry
- Thai Green Curry
- Japanese Chicken Katsu Curry
- Jamaican Goat Curry
- Malaysian Laksa Curry
- Indian Paneer Tikka Masala
- Sri Lankan Fish Curry
- Bangladeshi Beef Curry
- South African Bunny Chow
- Burmese Coconut Chicken Curry
- Pakistani Nihari Curry
- Indonesian Rendang Curry
- Caribbean Chicken Curry
- Ethiopian Doro Wat Curry
- British Chicken Tikka Masala
- Indian Lamb Rogan Josh
- Vietnamese Chicken Curry
- Thai Massaman Curry
- Nepalese Chicken Momo Curry
- Fijian Coconut Fish Curry
- Mauritian Octopus Curry
- Malaysian Nyonya Curry
- Trinidadian Duck Curry
- Afghan Lamb Korma
- Indian Chana Masala
- Filipino Kare-Kare Curry
- Nigerian Goat Curry
- Singaporean Fish Head Curry
- South Indian Chettinad Chicken Curry
- Tibetan Beef Curry
- Cambodian Amok Curry
- Bangladeshi Chicken Rezala
- Indian Malabar Prawn Curry
- Bhutanese Ema Datshi Curry
- Seychellois Coconut Fish Curry

- Maldivian Fish Curry
- Indian Aloo Gobi Curry
- Thai Red Curry with Duck
- Jamaican Vegetable Curry
- Kenyan Nyama Choma Curry
- Indian Egg Curry
- Ugandan Peanut Curry
- Omani Chicken Majboos Curry
- Indian Bhindi Masala Curry
- Indonesian Gulai Ayam Curry
- Indian Mushroom Curry
- Ethiopian Shiro Wat Curry
- Indian Dal Tadka Curry
- Malagasy Romazava Curry
- Indian Prawn Vindaloo

Indian Butter Chicken Curry

Ingredients:

- 500g chicken, cut into chunks
- 1 cup yogurt
- 2 tbsp lemon juice
- 2 tbsp ginger-garlic paste
- 2 tsp garam masala
- 1 tsp turmeric
- 2 tsp chili powder
- 4 tbsp butter
- 1 onion, finely chopped
- 3 tomatoes, pureed
- 1 cup cream
- 1 tsp fenugreek leaves
- Salt to taste
- Fresh cilantro for garnish

Instructions:

1. Marinate chicken with yogurt, lemon juice, ginger-garlic paste, garam masala, turmeric, chili powder, and salt for 2 hours.
2. Sauté onions in butter, add marinated chicken, and cook until browned.
3. Add tomato puree and simmer until chicken is cooked through.
4. Stir in cream, fenugreek leaves, and simmer for 5 minutes.
5. Garnish with cilantro and serve.

Thai Green Curry

Ingredients:

- 500g chicken, sliced
- 1 tbsp green curry paste
- 400ml coconut milk
- 2 cups mixed vegetables
- 1 tbsp fish sauce
- 1 tsp sugar
- Fresh basil leaves
- 1 red chili, sliced
- Salt to taste

Instructions:

1. Sauté green curry paste in a little coconut milk until fragrant.
2. Add chicken and cook until done.
3. Add remaining coconut milk, vegetables, fish sauce, sugar, and simmer until vegetables are tender.
4. Garnish with basil and red chili, and serve.

Japanese Chicken Katsu Curry

Ingredients:

- 2 chicken breasts
- 1 cup panko breadcrumbs
- 1 egg, beaten
- 1 cup flour
- Oil for frying
- 2 cups cooked rice
- 1 onion, sliced
- 1 carrot, sliced
- 2 potatoes, diced
- 2 tbsp curry powder
- 3 cups chicken stock
- 1 tbsp soy sauce

Instructions:

1. Coat chicken in flour, dip in egg, and coat with breadcrumbs. Fry until golden.
2. Sauté onion, carrot, and potatoes. Add curry powder, stock, soy sauce, and simmer until vegetables are tender.
3. Serve fried chicken over rice with curry sauce.

Jamaican Goat Curry

Ingredients:

- 1kg goat meat, cubed
- 2 onions, chopped
- 4 garlic cloves, minced
- 2 tbsp curry powder
- 1 tsp turmeric
- 2 cups coconut milk
- 2 potatoes, diced
- 2 carrots, diced
- 1 Scotch bonnet pepper
- Fresh thyme sprigs
- Salt to taste

Instructions:

1. Brown goat meat, then sauté onions and garlic.
2. Add curry powder, turmeric, coconut milk, potatoes, carrots, Scotch bonnet pepper, thyme, and simmer until meat is tender.
3. Serve hot.

Malaysian Laksa Curry

Ingredients:

- 400g rice noodles
- 2 tbsp laksa paste
- 400ml coconut milk
- 2 cups chicken stock
- 1 chicken breast, sliced
- 1 cup shrimp
- 1 cup bean sprouts
- Fresh cilantro
- Lime wedges

Instructions:

1. Cook rice noodles and set aside.
2. Sauté laksa paste, add coconut milk, stock, chicken, and simmer.
3. Add shrimp and bean sprouts, cook until done.
4. Serve over noodles, garnish with cilantro and lime.

Indian Paneer Tikka Masala

Ingredients:

- 250g paneer, cubed
- 1 cup yogurt
- 1 tbsp tandoori masala
- 1 onion, chopped
- 2 tomatoes, pureed
- 1 tbsp ginger-garlic paste
- 1 tsp cumin
- 1 tsp turmeric
- 1 cup cream
- Fresh cilantro

Instructions:

1. Marinate paneer in yogurt and tandoori masala for 1 hour.
2. Sauté onions, add ginger-garlic paste, cumin, turmeric, and cook.
3. Add tomato puree, cook until thick, add cream.
4. Add paneer, simmer for 5 minutes, garnish with cilantro.

Sri Lankan Fish Curry

Ingredients:

- 500g fish fillets
- 2 onions, chopped
- 3 garlic cloves, minced
- 2 tbsp curry powder
- 1 cup coconut milk
- 1 cup water
- 1 tomato, chopped
- 1 green chili, sliced
- Fresh curry leaves
- Salt to taste

Instructions:

1. Sauté onions, garlic, curry powder.
2. Add coconut milk, water, tomato, green chili, curry leaves.
3. Add fish, simmer until cooked. Serve hot.

Bangladeshi Beef Curry

Ingredients:

- 1kg beef, cubed
- 2 onions, chopped
- 4 garlic cloves, minced
- 2 tbsp mustard oil
- 1 tbsp turmeric
- 1 tbsp chili powder
- 1 tbsp cumin
- 2 tomatoes, chopped
- 1 cup water
- Salt to taste

Instructions:

1. Sauté onions, garlic in mustard oil.
2. Add spices, beef, cook until browned.
3. Add tomatoes, water, simmer until beef is tender. Serve hot.

South African Bunny Chow

Ingredients:

- 500g beef or lamb, cubed
- 2 onions, chopped
- 4 garlic cloves, minced
- 2 tbsp curry powder
- 1 cup water
- 1 loaf of bread
- Fresh cilantro

Instructions:

1. Sauté onions, garlic, add meat, cook until browned.
2. Add curry powder, water, simmer until meat is tender.
3. Hollow out the bread, fill with curry, garnish with cilantro.

Burmese Coconut Chicken Curry

Ingredients:

- 500g chicken, sliced
- 2 onions, chopped
- 4 garlic cloves, minced
- 2 tbsp curry powder
- 1 cup coconut milk
- 1 cup water
- Fresh cilantro
- Salt to taste

Instructions:

1. Sauté onions, garlic, add chicken, cook until browned.
2. Add curry powder, coconut milk, water, simmer until chicken is cooked.
3. Garnish with cilantro, serve hot.

Pakistani Nihari Curry

Ingredients:

- 1kg beef shank
- 2 onions, sliced
- 2 tbsp ginger-garlic paste
- 2 tbsp Nihari masala
- 1/4 cup wheat flour
- 6 cups water
- 1/4 cup oil
- Salt to taste
- Fresh cilantro, sliced ginger, and green chilies for garnish

Instructions:

1. Heat oil, sauté onions, add ginger-garlic paste, and cook.
2. Add beef, Nihari masala, salt, and cook until meat is browned.
3. Add water, cover, and simmer for several hours until meat is tender.
4. Dissolve wheat flour in water, add to curry to thicken, and simmer.
5. Garnish with cilantro, ginger, and green chilies before serving.

Indonesian Rendang Curry

Ingredients:

- 1kg beef, cubed
- 3 onions, chopped
- 3 garlic cloves, minced
- 2 tbsp rendang paste
- 400ml coconut milk
- 2 cups water
- 1 tbsp tamarind paste
- 1 stalk lemongrass
- Salt to taste

Instructions:

1. Sauté onions, garlic, add rendang paste, and cook until fragrant.
2. Add beef, coconut milk, water, tamarind paste, and lemongrass.
3. Simmer on low heat for 3-4 hours until beef is tender and sauce is thick.
4. Serve hot with rice.

Caribbean Chicken Curry

Ingredients:

- 500g chicken, cut into chunks
- 2 onions, chopped
- 4 garlic cloves, minced
- 2 tbsp Caribbean curry powder
- 1 cup coconut milk
- 1 cup water
- 1 sweet potato, diced
- 1 red bell pepper, diced
- Fresh cilantro
- Salt to taste

Instructions:

1. Sauté onions, garlic, add curry powder, and cook until fragrant.
2. Add chicken, coconut milk, water, sweet potato, bell pepper, and simmer until chicken is cooked and vegetables are tender.
3. Garnish with cilantro and serve.

Ethiopian Doro Wat Curry

Ingredients:

- 6 chicken drumsticks
- 2 onions, finely chopped
- 3 garlic cloves, minced
- 2 tbsp berbere spice mix
- 2 tbsp tomato paste
- 2 cups chicken stock
- 4 boiled eggs
- 1/4 cup oil
- Salt to taste

Instructions:

1. Sauté onions in oil until caramelized.
2. Add garlic, berbere spice, tomato paste, and cook for 5 minutes.
3. Add chicken and stock, simmer until chicken is tender.
4. Add boiled eggs and simmer for another 10 minutes.
5. Serve hot with injera or rice.

British Chicken Tikka Masala

Ingredients:

- 500g chicken, cubed
- 1 cup yogurt
- 2 tbsp tikka masala spice mix
- 1 onion, chopped
- 2 tomatoes, pureed
- 1 cup cream
- 1 tbsp butter
- Salt to taste
- Fresh cilantro for garnish

Instructions:

1. Marinate chicken in yogurt and tikka masala spice mix for 2 hours.
2. Sauté onions in butter, add marinated chicken, and cook until browned.
3. Add tomato puree, cook until thick, then add cream.
4. Simmer for 5 minutes, garnish with cilantro, and serve.

Indian Lamb Rogan Josh

Ingredients:

- 1kg lamb, cubed
- 2 onions, chopped
- 3 garlic cloves, minced
- 2 tbsp Rogan Josh spice mix
- 2 cups yogurt
- 2 cups water
- Salt to taste
- Fresh cilantro for garnish

Instructions:

1. Sauté onions, garlic, add lamb, and cook until browned.
2. Add Rogan Josh spice mix, yogurt, water, and simmer until lamb is tender.
3. Garnish with cilantro and serve hot.

Vietnamese Chicken Curry

Ingredients:

- 500g chicken, cut into chunks
- 2 onions, chopped
- 2 garlic cloves, minced
- 2 tbsp curry powder
- 1 cup coconut milk
- 2 cups chicken stock
- 2 potatoes, diced
- 2 carrots, sliced
- Fresh cilantro
- Salt to taste

Instructions:

1. Sauté onions, garlic, add curry powder, and cook until fragrant.
2. Add chicken, coconut milk, stock, potatoes, carrots, and simmer until chicken is cooked and vegetables are tender.
3. Garnish with cilantro and serve.

Thai Massaman Curry

Ingredients:

- 500g beef or chicken, cubed
- 2 onions, chopped
- 2 tbsp Massaman curry paste
- 400ml coconut milk
- 2 cups water
- 2 potatoes, diced
- 1/4 cup peanuts
- 1 tbsp tamarind paste
- Salt to taste

Instructions:

1. Sauté onions, add Massaman curry paste, and cook until fragrant.
2. Add beef or chicken, coconut milk, water, potatoes, and simmer until meat is tender.
3. Add peanuts, tamarind paste, and simmer for another 10 minutes.
4. Serve hot with rice.

Nepalese Chicken Momo Curry

Ingredients:

- 500g chicken mince
- 2 onions, chopped
- 2 garlic cloves, minced
- 1 tbsp ginger paste
- 1 tbsp curry powder
- 2 cups chicken stock
- 1 cup tomato puree
- Fresh cilantro
- Salt to taste

Instructions:

1. Sauté onions, garlic, ginger, and add chicken mince, cooking until browned.
2. Add curry powder, stock, tomato puree, and simmer until sauce thickens.
3. Serve over steamed momos and garnish with cilantro.

Fijian Coconut Fish Curry

Ingredients:

- 500g white fish fillets, cut into chunks
- 1 onion, chopped
- 3 garlic cloves, minced
- 2 tbsp curry powder
- 1 cup coconut milk
- 1 cup water
- 1 tsp turmeric
- 1 tbsp lemon juice
- Fresh cilantro
- Salt to taste

Instructions:

1. Sauté onions and garlic until softened.
2. Add curry powder, turmeric, and cook for 2 minutes.
3. Add fish, coconut milk, water, and simmer until fish is cooked.
4. Add lemon juice, garnish with cilantro, and serve.

Mauritian Octopus Curry

Ingredients:

- 500g octopus, cleaned and chopped
- 2 onions, chopped
- 2 garlic cloves, minced
- 2 tbsp curry powder
- 2 cups water
- 1 cup coconut milk
- 1 tbsp tomato paste
- Fresh cilantro
- Salt to taste

Instructions:

1. Sauté onions and garlic, add curry powder, and cook until fragrant.
2. Add octopus, tomato paste, water, coconut milk, and simmer until octopus is tender.
3. Garnish with cilantro and serve.

Malaysian Nyonya Curry

Ingredients:

- 500g chicken, cut into chunks
- 2 onions, chopped
- 3 garlic cloves, minced
- 2 tbsp Nyonya curry paste
- 1 cup coconut milk
- 2 cups water
- 1 tbsp tamarind paste
- Fresh cilantro
- Salt to taste

Instructions:

1. Sauté onions and garlic, add Nyonya curry paste, and cook until fragrant.
2. Add chicken, coconut milk, water, tamarind paste, and simmer until chicken is cooked.
3. Garnish with cilantro and serve.

Trinidadian Duck Curry

Ingredients:

- 1kg duck, cut into chunks
- 2 onions, chopped
- 3 garlic cloves, minced
- 2 tbsp curry powder
- 2 cups water
- 1 tbsp tamarind paste
- Fresh cilantro
- Salt to taste

Instructions:

1. Sauté onions and garlic, add curry powder, and cook until fragrant.
2. Add duck, water, tamarind paste, and simmer until duck is tender.
3. Garnish with cilantro and serve.

Afghan Lamb Korma

Ingredients:

- 1kg lamb, cubed
- 2 onions, chopped
- 3 garlic cloves, minced
- 2 tbsp korma spice mix
- 1 cup yogurt
- 2 cups water
- Fresh cilantro
- Salt to taste

Instructions:

1. Sauté onions and garlic, add lamb, and cook until browned.
2. Add korma spice mix, yogurt, water, and simmer until lamb is tender.
3. Garnish with cilantro and serve.

Indian Chana Masala

Ingredients:

- 2 cups chickpeas, cooked
- 1 onion, chopped
- 3 garlic cloves, minced
- 2 tbsp chana masala spice mix
- 1 cup tomato puree
- 1 cup water
- Fresh cilantro
- Salt to taste

Instructions:

1. Sauté onions and garlic, add chana masala spice mix, and cook until fragrant.
2. Add chickpeas, tomato puree, water, and simmer for 20 minutes.
3. Garnish with cilantro and serve.

Filipino Kare-Kare Curry

Ingredients:

- 500g beef, cubed
- 1 onion, chopped
- 3 garlic cloves, minced
- 2 tbsp peanut butter
- 1 cup coconut milk
- 2 cups water
- 1 tbsp fish sauce
- Fresh cilantro
- Salt to taste

Instructions:

1. Sauté onions and garlic, add beef, and cook until browned.
2. Add peanut butter, coconut milk, water, fish sauce, and simmer until beef is tender.
3. Garnish with cilantro and serve.

Nigerian Goat Curry

Ingredients:

- 1kg goat meat, cubed
- 2 onions, chopped
- 3 garlic cloves, minced
- 2 tbsp curry powder
- 2 cups water
- 1 cup coconut milk
- Fresh cilantro
- Salt to taste

Instructions:

1. Sauté onions and garlic, add goat meat, and cook until browned.
2. Add curry powder, water, coconut milk, and simmer until goat is tender.
3. Garnish with cilantro and serve.

Singaporean Fish Head Curry

Ingredients:

- 1 large fish head, cleaned
- 2 onions, chopped
- 3 garlic cloves, minced
- 2 tbsp curry powder
- 1 cup coconut milk
- 2 cups water
- 1 tbsp tamarind paste
- Fresh cilantro
- Salt to taste

Instructions:

1. Sauté onions and garlic, add curry powder, and cook until fragrant.
2. Add fish head, water, coconut milk, tamarind paste, and simmer until fish head is cooked.
3. Garnish with cilantro and serve.

South Indian Chettinad Chicken Curry

Ingredients:

- 500g chicken, cut into chunks
- 2 onions, chopped
- 3 garlic cloves, minced
- 2 tbsp Chettinad spice mix
- 1 cup tomato puree
- 2 cups water
- Fresh cilantro
- Salt to taste

Instructions:

1. Sauté onions and garlic, add Chettinad spice mix, and cook until fragrant.
2. Add chicken, tomato puree, water, and simmer until chicken is cooked.
3. Garnish with cilantro and serve.

Tibetan Beef Curry

Ingredients:

- 500g beef, cubed
- 2 onions, chopped
- 3 garlic cloves, minced
- 2 tbsp curry powder
- 2 cups water
- 1 cup tomato puree
- Fresh cilantro
- Salt to taste

Instructions:

1. Sauté onions and garlic, add beef, and cook until browned.
2. Add curry powder, tomato puree, water, and simmer until beef is tender.
3. Garnish with cilantro and serve.

Cambodian Amok Curry

Ingredients:

- 500g fish fillets, cut into chunks
- 1 onion, chopped
- 2 tbsp Amok curry paste
- 1 cup coconut milk
- 1 cup water
- 1 tbsp fish sauce
- 1 tbsp lime juice
- Fresh cilantro
- Salt to taste

Instructions:

1. Sauté onions until softened, then add Amok curry paste and cook until fragrant.
2. Add fish, coconut milk, water, fish sauce, and simmer until fish is tender.
3. Stir in lime juice and garnish with cilantro. Serve with rice.

Bangladeshi Chicken Rezala

Ingredients:

- 500g chicken, cut into pieces
- 2 onions, chopped
- 2 tbsp ginger-garlic paste
- 1 cup yogurt
- 2 tbsp cream
- 1 tbsp ground almonds
- 1 tsp garam masala
- 2 cups water
- Fresh cilantro
- Salt to taste

Instructions:

1. Sauté onions and ginger-garlic paste until golden.
2. Add chicken, yogurt, cream, almonds, and garam masala. Cook for 10 minutes.
3. Add water, simmer until chicken is cooked, and garnish with cilantro. Serve with rice.

Indian Malabar Prawn Curry

Ingredients:

- 500g prawns, peeled and deveined
- 1 onion, chopped
- 3 garlic cloves, minced
- 1 tbsp ginger, minced
- 2 tbsp Malabar curry paste
- 1 cup coconut milk
- 1 cup water
- Fresh cilantro
- Salt to taste

Instructions:

1. Sauté onions, garlic, and ginger until fragrant. Add Malabar curry paste and cook for 2 minutes.
2. Add prawns, coconut milk, and water. Simmer until prawns are cooked.
3. Garnish with cilantro and serve with rice.

Bhutanese Ema Datshi Curry

Ingredients:

- 500g green chilies, sliced
- 2 onions, chopped
- 2 tomatoes, chopped
- 1 cup cheese (e.g., Bhutanese cheese or paneer)
- 1 cup coconut milk
- 1 tbsp butter
- Fresh cilantro
- Salt to taste

Instructions:

1. Sauté onions, tomatoes, and green chilies in butter until softened.
2. Add cheese and coconut milk, cook for 5 minutes until cheese melts.
3. Garnish with cilantro and serve with rice.

Seychellois Coconut Fish Curry

Ingredients:

- 500g fish fillets, cut into chunks
- 1 onion, chopped
- 3 garlic cloves, minced
- 1 tbsp curry powder
- 1 cup coconut milk
- 1 cup water
- Fresh cilantro
- Salt to taste

Instructions:

1. Sauté onions and garlic until softened. Add curry powder and cook until fragrant.
2. Add fish, coconut milk, and water. Simmer until fish is cooked.
3. Garnish with cilantro and serve with rice.

Maldivian Fish Curry

Ingredients:

- 500g fish, cut into pieces
- 2 onions, chopped
- 3 garlic cloves, minced
- 1 tbsp curry powder
- 1 cup coconut milk
- 1 cup water
- Fresh cilantro
- Salt to taste

Instructions:

1. Sauté onions and garlic until softened. Add curry powder and cook for 2 minutes.
2. Add fish, coconut milk, and water. Simmer until fish is cooked.
3. Garnish with cilantro and serve.

Indian Aloo Gobi Curry

Ingredients:

- 2 potatoes, peeled and cubed
- 1 cauliflower, cut into florets
- 2 onions, chopped
- 3 garlic cloves, minced
- 1 tbsp curry powder
- 1 cup tomato puree
- Fresh cilantro
- Salt to taste

Instructions:

1. Sauté onions and garlic until softened. Add curry powder and cook until fragrant.
2. Add potatoes, cauliflower, tomato puree, and simmer until vegetables are tender.
3. Garnish with cilantro and serve with rice or naan.

Thai Red Curry with Duck

Ingredients:

- 500g duck breast, sliced
- 2 onions, chopped
- 3 garlic cloves, minced
- 2 tbsp red curry paste
- 1 cup coconut milk
- 1 cup water
- Fresh basil
- Salt to taste

Instructions:

1. Sauté onions and garlic until softened. Add red curry paste and cook for 2 minutes.
2. Add duck, coconut milk, and water. Simmer until duck is cooked.
3. Garnish with fresh basil and serve with rice.

Jamaican Vegetable Curry

Ingredients:

- 1 cup carrots, chopped
- 1 cup potatoes, cubed
- 1 cup bell peppers, chopped
- 1 cup peas
- 2 onions, chopped
- 3 garlic cloves, minced
- 2 tbsp curry powder
- 1 cup coconut milk
- Fresh cilantro
- Salt to taste

Instructions:

1. Sauté onions and garlic until softened. Add curry powder and cook for 2 minutes.
2. Add carrots, potatoes, bell peppers, peas, and coconut milk. Simmer until vegetables are tender.
3. Garnish with cilantro and serve with rice.

Kenyan Nyama Choma Curry

Ingredients:

- 500g beef or lamb, cubed
- 2 onions, chopped
- 3 garlic cloves, minced
- 2 tbsp ginger, minced
- 1 tbsp curry powder
- 1 tbsp ground coriander
- 1 tbsp ground cumin
- 1 cup tomato puree
- 1 cup water
- Fresh cilantro
- Salt to taste

Instructions:

1. Sauté onions, garlic, and ginger until fragrant.
2. Add curry powder, coriander, and cumin. Cook for 2 minutes.
3. Add beef or lamb, tomato puree, and water. Simmer until meat is tender.
4. Garnish with fresh cilantro and serve with rice or ugali.

Indian Egg Curry

Ingredients:

- 6 boiled eggs, peeled
- 2 onions, chopped
- 3 garlic cloves, minced
- 1 tbsp ginger, minced
- 1 tbsp curry powder
- 1 tsp turmeric powder
- 1 cup tomato puree
- 1 cup coconut milk
- Fresh cilantro
- Salt to taste

Instructions:

1. Sauté onions, garlic, and ginger until golden brown.
2. Add curry powder, turmeric, and cook for 2 minutes.
3. Add tomato puree, coconut milk, and simmer until sauce thickens.
4. Add boiled eggs, coat them with the curry, and cook for 5 more minutes.
5. Garnish with cilantro and serve with rice or roti.

Ugandan Peanut Curry

Ingredients:

- 1 cup peanuts, ground into a paste
- 2 onions, chopped
- 3 garlic cloves, minced
- 1 tbsp ginger, minced
- 1 tbsp curry powder
- 2 tomatoes, chopped
- 1 cup coconut milk
- Fresh cilantro
- Salt to taste

Instructions:

1. Sauté onions, garlic, and ginger until fragrant.
2. Add curry powder and cook for 2 minutes.
3. Stir in tomatoes, peanuts, and coconut milk. Simmer for 10 minutes until thickened.
4. Garnish with cilantro and serve with rice or chapati.

Omani Chicken Majboos Curry

Ingredients:

- 500g chicken, cut into pieces
- 2 onions, chopped
- 3 garlic cloves, minced
- 1 tbsp ginger, minced
- 2 tbsp Majboos spice mix (or use a combination of cinnamon, cumin, coriander, and turmeric)
- 1 cup tomato puree
- 1 cup chicken stock
- Fresh cilantro
- Salt to taste

Instructions:

1. Sauté onions, garlic, and ginger until golden.
2. Add Majboos spice mix and cook for 2 minutes.
3. Add chicken, tomato puree, and chicken stock. Simmer until chicken is cooked.
4. Garnish with fresh cilantro and serve with rice.

Indian Bhindi Masala Curry

Ingredients:

- 500g okra (bhindi), sliced
- 2 onions, chopped
- 3 garlic cloves, minced
- 1 tbsp ginger, minced
- 1 tsp turmeric powder
- 1 tsp ground cumin
- 1 tsp garam masala
- 2 tomatoes, chopped
- Fresh cilantro
- Salt to taste

Instructions:

1. Sauté onions, garlic, and ginger until softened.
2. Add turmeric, cumin, and garam masala, cooking for 2 minutes.
3. Add chopped tomatoes and simmer for 5 minutes.
4. Add okra and cook until tender, stirring occasionally.
5. Garnish with cilantro and serve with roti or rice.

Indonesian Gulai Ayam Curry

Ingredients:

- 500g chicken, cut into pieces
- 2 onions, chopped
- 3 garlic cloves, minced
- 1 tbsp ginger, minced
- 1 tbsp turmeric powder
- 1 tbsp curry powder
- 1 cup coconut milk
- 1 cup water
- Fresh cilantro
- Salt to taste

Instructions:

1. Sauté onions, garlic, and ginger until golden.
2. Add turmeric and curry powder, cooking for 2 minutes.
3. Add chicken, coconut milk, and water. Simmer until chicken is tender.
4. Garnish with cilantro and serve with steamed rice.

Indian Mushroom Curry

Ingredients:

- 500g mushrooms, sliced
- 2 onions, chopped
- 3 garlic cloves, minced
- 1 tbsp ginger, minced
- 1 tbsp curry powder
- 1 tsp cumin seeds
- 1 tsp turmeric powder
- 1 cup tomato puree
- 1/2 cup coconut milk
- Fresh cilantro
- Salt to taste

Instructions:

1. Sauté onions, garlic, and ginger in oil until softened.
2. Add cumin seeds, curry powder, and turmeric, and cook for 2 minutes.
3. Add mushrooms and cook until tender.
4. Stir in tomato puree and coconut milk, simmering for 10 minutes.
5. Garnish with cilantro and serve with rice or roti.

Ethiopian Shiro Wat Curry

Ingredients:

- 1 cup chickpea flour (shiro powder)
- 2 onions, chopped
- 3 garlic cloves, minced
- 1 tbsp ginger, minced
- 1 tbsp berbere spice mix
- 1 tbsp turmeric powder
- 2 cups vegetable broth
- 1/2 cup tomato puree
- Fresh cilantro
- Salt to taste

Instructions:

1. Sauté onions, garlic, and ginger in oil until golden brown.
2. Add berbere spice mix and turmeric, and cook for 2 minutes.
3. Stir in chickpea flour, vegetable broth, and tomato puree. Simmer for 15 minutes.
4. Garnish with fresh cilantro and serve with injera or rice.

Indian Dal Tadka Curry

Ingredients:

- 1 cup split yellow lentils (toor dal)
- 2 onions, chopped
- 3 garlic cloves, minced
- 1 tbsp ginger, minced
- 1 tsp cumin seeds
- 1/2 tsp turmeric powder
- 1 tsp garam masala
- 2 tomatoes, chopped
- Fresh cilantro
- Salt to taste

Instructions:

1. Cook the lentils in water until tender, then set aside.
2. Sauté onions, garlic, and ginger in oil until softened.
3. Add cumin seeds, turmeric, and garam masala. Cook for 2 minutes.
4. Add tomatoes, cooking until they soften, then mix in cooked lentils.
5. Simmer for 10 minutes, garnish with cilantro, and serve with rice or roti.

Malagasy Romazava Curry

Ingredients:

- 500g beef or chicken, cut into pieces
- 2 onions, chopped
- 3 garlic cloves, minced
- 1 tbsp ginger, minced
- 1 tbsp turmeric powder
- 1 tsp cumin seeds
- 2 cups beef or vegetable broth
- 1 bunch of spinach or collard greens, chopped
- Salt to taste

Instructions:

1. Sauté onions, garlic, and ginger in oil until golden.
2. Add turmeric and cumin, cooking for 2 minutes.
3. Add beef or chicken, and cook until browned.
4. Pour in broth and simmer until the meat is tender.
5. Add greens and cook for an additional 10 minutes. Season with salt and serve with rice.

Indian Prawn Vindaloo

Ingredients:

- 500g prawns, peeled and deveined
- 2 onions, chopped
- 3 garlic cloves, minced
- 1 tbsp ginger, minced
- 1 tbsp vindaloo spice mix (or a combination of cumin, coriander, turmeric, and chili powder)
- 1/2 cup vinegar
- 1/2 cup tomato puree
- 1/2 cup coconut milk
- Fresh cilantro
- Salt to taste

Instructions:

1. Sauté onions, garlic, and ginger in oil until softened.
2. Add vindaloo spice mix and cook for 2 minutes.
3. Stir in vinegar, tomato puree, and coconut milk, simmering for 5 minutes.
4. Add prawns and cook until pink and cooked through.
5. Garnish with fresh cilantro and serve with rice or naan.

www.ingramcontent.com/pod-product-compliance
Lightning Source LLC
LaVergne TN
LVHW081507060526
838201LV00056BA/2985